Walk w...

For many of us prayer and meditation are just other
things to do, finding off the busy schedule, rather than an
oasis of peace and quiet to refresh and renew us as it should
be at times.

"I don't have the time" is the commonest response to thoughts
about more prayer and meditation. As much as we can argue that
we should make the time, in theory it often just doesn't work.

Most of us find it easy to take time out to pray for the things we
want or are troubled about. Prayers come tripping off our
tongues then as easy as speaking to a friend when faced with a
crisis. But taking time out to meditate on the Passion of Jesus is a
completely different matter, especially during Lent on the lead up
to Easter, as there are always too many distractions around us.

Why not take the Stations of the Cross one by one and use
them in sequence throughout Lent, daily or weekly? There is a
message to be read in each Station which can be applied to
everyday living which can make that message as personal as you
wish.

Copyright © Redemptorist Publications
A Registered Charity limited by guarantee
Registered in England 3261721

First Printing   January 1998

Text: Catriona Davidson
Design: Roger Smith

ISBN 0 85231 173 7

Printed by:
Knight and Willson Limited Leeds LS11 5SF

Redemptorist
PUBLICATIONS

Alphonsus House Chawton Hampshire GU34 3HQ
Telephone: 01420 88222 Fax: 01420 88805
rp@redempt.org   http://www.redempt.org

A registered Charity limited by guarantee. Registered in England 3261721

Before slandering someone else, look to yourself.

This is the allotted day, Jesus' fate is already determined and he cannot alter it. He has been sentenced to death, and there is nowhere to hide.

None of us can truly relate to Jesus being led away to be crucified. It is far too severe a sentence for us to comprehend. But many of us do feel sentenced at one time or another in our lives.

Sometimes we spend our lives looking at other people's failures, misfortunes, or mistakes, and make it our business to judge. When we meet up with friends it gives us something to talk about, what Mary so and so down the road is saying and doing and before long we are discussing her character in depth and determining whether she should or shouldn't be doing what she is doing. We refer to it as gossip and it can take up a large proportion of our socialising time.

Even sitcom soaps and TV shows incorporate such gossip into their scripts, with sometimes the whole story line revolving around the gossip of one individual person. We find it funny, because we can relate to it ourselves, it's part of our everyday lives.

But when we become the centre of gossip, the tables are turned and we don't like it at all. We don't like people discussing our every movements and passing judgement on us.

This is because we are then forced to face the truth about ourselves and often it's not too rosy a picture. Perhaps we could spend more time looking at our own faults, weaknesses and character before blackening another person.

PUTTING IT INTO PRACTICE:
1. Try not to be cruel or uncharitable to others.
2. Before criticising others, be more self-critical.
3. Learn to take criticism from others more.
4. Maybe write letters to prisoners of Conscience, or visit those in prison.

Accepting your own personal cross, taking on board personal responsibility.

His fate is inevitable but Jesus is still afraid of what is to come. Nevertheless he accepts his cross.

Everyone has their own personal cross in life be it from working under someone you don't like, to having to care for an old and difficult relative on a permanent basis.

For some of us those crosses can be very real. Having a partner walk out of a relationship, working under a slave driver, having your children turn against you or go their separate ways, experiencing loss of any kind are crosses to be born. Perhaps those who feel they have the hardest cross to bear are those who have a severe illness. They feel that their life has been taken out of their hands and they have no control over the path they take.

If not illness, you could relate this station to someone who has been faced with widowhood or a child dying. Their life has suddenly taken a turn for the worse, life will no longer seem normal, and it will be hard to have the strength to go on when the way ahead looks so bleak.

Those that have an addiction, be it cigarettes or hard drugs, have their cross to bear, especially those living with them, trying to pick up the pieces. But for some of us our crosses can be quite trivial, it can be as simple as having to put up with someone who gets on our nerves, experiencing a disappointment in our lives, or having to study for exams.

The message in this station is acceptance. This certainly doesn't mean making yourself a door mat, allowing others to take advantage. But there are times in our lives when it would serve us and others better if we accepted our cross and determined not to complain about it so much.

PUTTING IT INTO PRACTICE:

1. Try to accept your own personal cross, don't grumble so much, and rejoice in your own good fortune, whatever that may be.
2. Bear your cross with grace, but don't allow others to take advantage.
3. Whilst accepting your cross make a point in taking time out for yourself each day.
4. Why not visit someone sick in hospital, many people in nursing homes have no visitors.

Don't be afraid to show weakness, learn to be humble.

The Son of God uses no superhuman powers and in a public display of weakness falls under the weight of the cross.

For most of us the hardest thing in life is to show humility especially to those we believe don't truly deserve it. In the fast world today where everyone is out to prove themselves to others, succeed, earn lots of money and live a comfortable life style the last thing we want to show each other is our weakness.

If we show our weakness to someone we immediately feel we are exposing our vulnerability, admitting we are a failure at something, and proving we are less of a person in the process. Unfortunately we do not see the showing of weakness as a sign of strength.

In the work place for example, more often than not we are too proud to ask for help in case we look stupid. Showing weakness can be as simple as admitting we don't understand something, can't do something, or are afraid of doing something. But it is only by admitting such weakness that we ever learn.

We can show our weakness even in our daily routine with other members of our family. It might be as simple as admitting we were wrong about something, need financial help, or have a problem that needs to be shared.

To show weakness is to show humility, to not allow yourself to become egotistical, to accept that there will always be someone who has more authority than yourself. Even if you cannot agree with everything that person says, for the most part, everyone has useful advice that should be listened to and quite often accepted and it doesn't make you less of a person to do so.

PUTTING IT INTO PRACTICE:
1. Don't be afraid to ask for help when you need it.
2. Try to admit you are in the wrong when you are.
3. Heed other's advice, and learn to listen what other's have to say even if you don't agree with them.

Don't be afraid to show emotion and love for others.

As Jesus turns to see his mother, their looks of love become as one.

In today's world it is extremely difficult not to be completely wrapped up in our own problems, and worries. Taking time out to think about others isn't always our first priority as we feel we have enough on our own plate.

Sometimes when we are surrounded by those we are closest to we are our most selfish. We believe that if they know and love us so well they of all people should be able to accept us, warts and all. If we are miserable, or bad tempered without even doing so deliberately we target all our pent up anger against them.

They weren't the instigators of our ill mood, but if they are our family or friends they should understand! The trouble is, we do this to the people we love all the time in our daily lives. Often the people we most dislike, are the people we treat most courteously, as we fear they wouldn't put up with us otherwise.

The answer isn't to be ourselves with everyone and let them get on with it, but simply to try and think about ourselves last. Instead we could try to consider other people's feelings and wishes first, even if it is only for just one day.

We shouldn't be afraid to show our love for the people who are the most important in our lives, for by giving of love in action we are losing nothing, and in the end we only stand to gain.

The hardest lesson is to try and be the same towards people whom or one reason or another we just don't take to, people that irritate and annoy us, and whose company we find a drag.

PUTTING IT INTO PRACTICE:
1. Put others first even if just for one day, even those you don't particularly like or get one with.
2. Allow someone to have their own way once in a while.
3. Show how much you love someone in action or deed.

5. SIMON OF CYRENE TAKES UP THE CROSS – RESPONSIBILITY & GRATITUDE

Be generous in your giving.

Jesus is crippled with pain, when suddenly an unwilling stranger is made to offer his help. But Jesus still turns and gives him a look of gratitude.

You've just settled down in front of the TV, with a mug of hot chocolate, some of your favourite biscuits and that epic film you've been looking forward to all week is just about to flash on screen when suddenly someone asks you to give them a lift, do some shopping, make a meal, tell the time, listen to a problem, the phone rings, in short someone needs your help.

If it was me, I might give that person the help they needed but more often than not, I would make heavy weather of it. I would make sure they knew just how inconvenient it was to do it just then, and how irritated I feel that I'm in no position to say no without looking and feeling selfish.

By the time I have helped that person, they no doubt wish they had never asked in the first place. Looking at it from the other side, how many of us want to smile sweetly and thank the person who pulls a face when asked to do something? The last person you want to show gratitude to is the person who makes it obvious they didn't want to do it in the first place.

The message of this Station is to be generous in your giving and give to those who deserve it.

PUTTING IT INTO PRACTICE:
1. Offer your help with good grace.
2. Be generous in your giving, in action and deed.
3. Give a person credit where it's due.
4. Don't take friendship for granted.

Don't be afraid to stand up for what's right.

Jesus stands an outcast among men. Brave Veronica pushes her way through the guards to wipe the blood and sweat from his face so he can see.

In society today when someone is ridiculing another, putting them down, making racist or defamatory comments, it is easier to keep quiet and say nothing even if our own blood is boiling and we feel they are grossly unfair in what they are saying.

We find it easier to go with the general consensus. We want to go with the crowd, not draw attention to ourselves, not be the odd one out, for if we do, we might become the focus for ridicule ourselves.

But if we see another person persecuted we know we should fly to their help, no matter how it may reverberate on ourselves. We should stand up for what is right, or at least what we believe to be right, even if we are mistaken.

People with their prejudices, to give them any credit at all, are at least being true to their own beliefs, however distorted they may be, we should be true to ours.

PUTTING IT INTO PRACTICE:
1. Learn to be rid of prejudice.
2. Stand up for others, even if it makes you look bad.
3. Maybe do some voluntary work, or look after a sick relative for a day.

Whatever you've failed to do once, pick up and start again.

> The weight of the cross proves too much for Jesus and once more he falls defeated to the ground.

Failure is one of the most difficult hurdles to overcome. It leads to loss of confidence making you believe you cannot succeed in the future.

If we find an exam easy, we have a good day at work, we often quite look forward to the next day, and go in with a singular determination to do even better. More often than not, that's exactly we do. Where there's a will, there's a way.

On the other hand, if we under achieve we immediately question the point of carrying on.

Failing at something can be as simple as arriving late for work more times than you can remember, doing badly in an exam, forgetting something important you were supposed to do. It could also mean failing an interview, driving test, not completing a course, or just anything you have put off for so long, you feel you can no longer make a start now.

That start could be doing the housework, getting in touch with an old friend, relative, visiting someone who you know is in need of your friendship, forgiving someone, it could even be that diet you've meant to do for so long.

It doesn't matter how trivial it may seem, it's the determination to pick up from where you last left off, and faced with the possibility of failure, still try once more. If at first you don't succeed, try, try, try again.

PUTTING IT INTO PRACTICE
1. Have another try at something you've failed at before.
2. Get in touch with an old friend or relative you've fallen out with.
3. Make a start on what you've been putting off for so long.

Learn to be loyal and steadfast to those you know and love.

As Jesus comes across the women of Jerusalem weeping for him he tells them not to weep for him but to weep for themselves and their children.

Loyalty is one of the most important things in our lives. We know that if we are in times of trouble, or need a shoulder to cry on, our friends are those we can always rely on.

The same is true, if not more so, of our family. They will stick with us through thick and thin, no matter what, as they love us. But such loyalty is sometimes hard to return.

Loyalty can be as simple as keeping a secret for someone, defending a friend in an argument, not believing gossip about a close friend of family member, or even giving support to someone we love though we know they are in the wrong.

To be loyal to someone means to stand by them, to always think the best of someone no matter what the circumstance. To believe there is good in everyone.

Loyalty is something we all hold precious . We all make many acquaintances in life, but it is always those we feel we can most trust that we believe to be our true friends.

Security is the most important thing in any relationship, we like to feel we can always rely on that person's support, whatever the situation may be. We most value genuine and sincere affection.

That is why the message here is to remember that we must always try to be loyal to whatever or whoever is important in our lives, be it our religion, our partner in life, or our friends.

PUTTING IT INTO PRACTICE:
1. Try to remain true and honest to all your friends.
2. Learn to tell the truth, whatever the circumstance.
3. Don't let someone down who is relying on you.
4. Don't denounce your faith, be proud of it.

Have patience for the addict who despairs of life.

Jesus falls to the ground one more time, and this time almost gives up hope that he can go on.

For those with real addictions, it must seem as though there will be no end to falling down. It is often something in their lives that has propelled them towards needing to take a substitute. They feel they have lost some quality of life and so need to substitute it with something else.

Often those addicted to alcohol, drink to forget. They want to block out all remembrance of what it is that pains them, what has made them despair of life, they want to escape into a warm make-believe world where everything seems cheerful and no-one can hurt them again. It works for them, but kills them or others who live with them first.

The same is true of any addiction, like pills or drugs it is the substitute for company, love, self respect, and hope. Those who are addicted are dependant on something that helps them make it through to the next day. They need something solid to look forward to, because all other hope of life has been lost. People only become dependant on something when they are lacking something else. Even those addicted to slimming put their bodies and minds through somersaults because they have lost respect for themselves and want desperately to become someone or something else which they believe will make them happy.

For those living with an addiction, the thought of living a normal life without a substitute to dull their pain, whatever it may be, is often too much to bear. The fear for them is the thought of never being able to get up again ever on their own.

PUTTING IT INTO PRACTICE:

1. Learn patience for the person who continually falls down making the same mistake.
2. Give encouragement and hope to those that despair of life.
3. Suggest going along with someone who needs help to a counsellor.
4. Give encouragement to those trying to kick a habit or addiction, don't continually chastise them when they don't succeed.

Learn not to be greedy, over-ambitious, or arrogant.

All his belongings are stripped from him, he is left, naked with nothing.

Today in the age of Lottery Fever, it is extremely difficult not to crave a windfall, imagine that extra house, large garden, swimming pool, or cruise around the Mediterranean.

Even those with money, real money, stake their bet, be it on the Grand National, the Lottery, or the local bingo. Everyone wants to be rich, because money stands for success and happiness, and we get greedy.

If we have a small win we immediately declare "My luck must be in" and then spend the amount we have just won on more chances of winning even more. We are never satisfied, we always want more. We are driven by greed.

But if it's not gambling then it's ambition in the work place. Society has become obsessed with money, and people are becoming more and more willing to put friendship, family and marriage on the line in their bid to put their ambition for earning lots of money first.

Frequently, people have no scruples about treating another person badly in the work place if it means promotion for themselves. The argument is "They would do the same if they were in my shoes", and more often than not, they are right.

It is important to learn to be more selfless, be happy with our lot and not constantly hunger for more money if we are comfortable. Stripping away all our worldly desires to focus on what is really important in life.

PUTTING IT INTO PRACTICE:
1. Learn to be happy with your lot.
2. Cut down on your spending, try not to be so frivolous with your money.
3. Don't let greed blind you into becoming ruthless with friends in the work place,.
4. Cut back on spending money on gambling, don't buy your lottery ticket one week, miss the bingo, or don't buy that cake.
5. Instead, give that money to charity.

Unable to move through duty or love.

Mercilessly they nail his frail body to the wood of the cross.

It is easy to feel and show sympathy for the tramp in the street who you feel has an unfair lot in life. But to feel sympathy for someone who you believe has only got themselves to blame for the position they find themselves in is near impossible. Often then, our hearts seem as hard as nails as we become resolute in determining not to show them any sympathy.

Having the time to feel sympathy or empathy for another often seems too much of an effort especially when engrossed in our problems of the day. Sometimes a friend will seek us out in their hour of need. Often than not all that person wants is for someone to listen to them, to share with them how they feel fixed or imprisoned in their lives.

This could relate to anyone who feels unable to move through duty or love. They feel fixed to their cross, pinioned to their fate. It could relate to a woman who remains with the husband who repeatedly beats her, for the children's sake, the wife or husband who sticks with their partner who repeatedly cheats on them or treats them badly.

It could also be a family forced to help one another through a rough period in their life even though they know the situation will never get any better. It may relate to parents who support their children, even when they do wrong, or who care for their sick or disabled child throughout his or her life, or day in day out care of an elderly relative.

Many people feel nailed to their cross at one time or another in their lives. The message is not to sit in judgement but be there to listen as a friend, and to be as sympathetic as possible.

PUTTING IT INTO PRACTICE:
1. Lend a sympathetic ear to someone who feels they are trapped and unhappy in life, even if you believe they have brought it upon themselves.
2. Why not offer your help as a Samaritan?
3. Don't allow yourself to be tied down to anything, take control of your life.

Learn to live in the present, take hope in the future.

Jesus bows his head and gives up his Spirit.

We all have good periods in our lives which we dread coming to an end. There are good days and bad days, and often when we have a good day we almost start looking over our shoulder wondering when the next bad day will dawn.

People need things to look forward to, occasions to work towards. It is for this reason we all take holidays, and count down the days until we finally have that break we have worked towards for so long.

It doesn't matter where we go, it could be Blackpool, Barbados, or the back garden, so long as it is something we can all look forward to. But almost as soon as we are enjoying our break we start thinking about when it will soon be over. We dread the good times coming to an end, and as it is something which will inevitably take place, it hangs over us like a dark black cloud.

The problem is many of us spend too much time living in the future, rather than the present. If we are not dreading what is to come we are wishing our lives away until the next happy occasion.

Many of us, can often see death as the dreadful inevitable. It happens to all of us, it's not the most comforting notion, and you can't escape it.

Death seems like an end to living, the good times coming to a close. But death can be seen as the release of the soul, a time when, however you want to comprehend it, you are at peace with your life as it is then, in the present. There is no longer a race for the finishing line, or something to dread, but peace.

And until then, that is how we should and must view life, being at peace with ourselves, living in the present.

PUTTING IT INTO PRACTICE:
1. Always believe the best is to come, but rejoice in the present.
2. Learn to just live each day.
3. Don't allow one bad day to overcloud the next.

Learn to let go of the past.

The lifeless body of Jesus is placed in the tender arms of Mary his mother.

Even if none of us have had to experience the great tragedy of losing a child we all know the desperate sorrow you feel when losing a member of the family, like a grandparent, a friend, or even a family pet.

Suddenly we are left with an empty shell, a cruel reminder of their great vitality for life, their talents, humour, character all gone. It can seem even more devastating if it's a small baby with his or her life before them or a youngster or teenager who was just starting to make their first real choices in life about who they wanted to be.

The obvious feeling, is what was the point. Why live to die? There is no answer that will adequately comfort anyone in that position. Everyone's bereavement is different from another's and everyone's pain is very different.

But often the will to go on living without that person seems impossible especially if a partner. We become dejected and lose all purpose in life. What's the point in going on?

Some people are faced with loneliness for the first time in their lives and a simple task of going to the shops on their own to buy some food can seem too much. They shrink into themselves and before long lose all self respect, and no longer look after themselves, they no longer have anything to live for.

This can apply to the parent who is no longer allowed to see their own children, even though they are alive and well and living their own separate lives. This station can also apply to those who are divorced and separated.

The over riding feeling for those experiencing bereavement in whatever way or form is one of being left desperately alone. They no longer have the will to live themselves. Life to them is loneliness.

PUTTING IT INTO PRACTICE:
1. **Forgive those who have hurt your feelings, let go of your bitterness.**
2. **Offer your help, or visit a friend or member of family who has lost someone close to them, make sure they are never left on their own.**
3. **Attempt to let go of the past and move on. Try not to bring your own pain into every conversation, take an interest in others.**

Learn to show respect to others.

They laid the body of Jesus in the tomb, and rolled the stone across the entrance.

No matter how much we love someone, when they have died and gone as every year goes by our memory of them fades even more, and it can seem very distressing.

People want to imagine them exactly as they were before they died. How they laughed, the colour of their eyes, the way their hair fell, everything. We want to remember everything about them so we feel as though we could just reach out and touch them.

We will often root out our latest photographs of them or if lucky enough will look at a video we have taken of them. We want to remember them and honour them in some way which is why we still remember their anniversaries, have Masses said for them, visit their grave and plant flowers as a mark of respect.

Often we have deep regrets when someone dies that we didn't tell them how much we loved and respected them. Perhaps the true message of this Station is to honour and respect not only those who have since died but those still living. We perhaps should show just as much honour and respect to those around us, the people we meet in our every day lives, friends, family and even strangers.

Showing such respect and honour can be as simple as curbing our tongue when we know we are about to be rude to someone, not feel prejudice against another's race or religion or preferences, and not be disrespectful to our parents.

In short, showing respect, even if we often don't agree with everything another person says, at least hear them out and be polite.

PUTTING IT INTO PRACTICE:

1. Show respect to those you both like and dislike in your work-place or social gatherings.
2. Pay your respects to a loved one who has died by visiting their grave.
3. Learn to respect and pay heed to even the advice and opinions of children.

Welcome new life, new circles of friends, new ways of life.

Three days later, the stone was rolled back from the tomb, he had risen from the dead.

In the early Church, the cross was seen as a sign of victory. Some Stations of the Cross now celebrate a 15th station to make this point.

By marking this last station we are acknowledging the reason for why Jesus went through the other Stations of the Cross, why he bore the suffering and pain, to give us the chance of new life, and to prove his power over death.

Sometimes it is very difficult for us to break with tradition. We know what we like and often we become set in our ways. Often we can become immovable and in so doing so alienate ourselves from others.

It can be as simple as not fully welcoming another member into your family circle, be it a new neighbour offering friendship, or a young person marrying into your close immediate circle, a child watching a parent taking a new wife or husband after being left widowed, or one religion finding difficulty in embracing another.

But this station can also relate to someone left alone, who has become so used to their own company they know and want no better. They shut out the outside world to feel secure in their own presence. The message is to reach out to others and make a brand new start in life.

In it's rawest sense it can mean an awakening, opening our eyes to what is around us and rejoicing in what we have, and life all around us.

PUTTING IT INTO PRACTICE:
1. Be welcoming to all you meet in life, invite the neighbours round for a cup of tea and a chat.
2. Join a new club, or group and meet new people.
3. Visit someone you know is lonely.
4. Put aside all prejudices and instead offer the hand of friendship.
5. Offer to baby-sit or help someone you know who has just had a baby.